HAVE NINE LIVES

Have Nine Lives

Tristan Buttigieg

MCMLXXVIII

New York ~ New Hope

HAVE NINE LIVES

Copyright © 2021 by Tristan Buttigieg.

All rights reserved. No part of this publication may be reproduced, distributed, or transmitted in any form or by any means, electronic, or mechanical, including photocopying, recording, or by information storage and retrieval system, without the prior written permission of the publisher.

For permission requests contact the publisher.

Copyright © Front Cover Images and Design by Tristan Buttigieg

Library of Congress Control Number: 2021935681

ISBN 978-0-932436-31-3 (Paperback Edition)

ISBN 978-0-932436-74-0 (Ebook Edition)

Published in the United States by Cykxbooks,

An imprint of Cykxbooks Publishers.

Cykx and associated logos are Trademarks and/or Registered Trademarks in the US Patent and Trademark Office and other countries. Marcas Registratas of Cykxincorp.

CYKXBOOKS

A Division of Cykxincorp,

P.O. Box 299

Lenox Hill Sta,

New York, NY 10021

cykxbooks@cykxincorp.com

Manufactured in the United States of America

1 2 3 4 5 6   CBP   26 25 24 23 22 21

Dedicated To Jack Lazarow

Contents

Line Up The Animals	13
Hero With A Thousand Faces	16
Nightmare Fuel	18
Bombay Sapphire	20
All With Wildflowers	22
Haiku 1	24
Low Hanging Fruit	25
Seasons of Conejo	27
Tears Don't Flow The Same In Space	29
The Humanoid Zoo	32
Tinderbox	34
Haiku 2	36
The Geisha Parade	37
Blue Ribbon Winner	39
Moonlighting @ Vogue	41
Haiku 3	43
Gentleman Dreaming	44

Same Moves As Eve	45
Burials In Bulgaria	47
Stickfiguree	48
Haiku 4	49
Powder Cake	50
Porcelain Twins	51
Metal Desk Furniture	53
Chalky Shale Cats	· 54
Foam Hole Rooms	56
Haiku 5	57
Lacuna Fortuna	58
Rainy Season In The Andes	59
Color It With Fire	61
In His Sunday Best	64
It's Only Good For Business	65
Haiku 6	67
Polishing The Marble	68
Sugar Raw	69
We Feast @ 3:08	71
Kilroy Was Here	72

It's Almost Funny	74
The Commodore's Shack	76
Saving Face	78
Haiku 7	79
Little White Shoes	80
Wind Chimes On The Far North Side	82
Our Usual Song	84
Choking Nickie's and Deep Eddie's	86
Fast Responder	88
Don't Cry Over Spilled Juice	89
Stick With Me Lazrow	90
Haiku 8	93
Portuguese Man O'War	94
The Great Circus Fire	95
Round-Topped Stella	97
Malady Melady	99
Mason's Ashtray	101
House at Hast	103
Extra Seville	104

Haiku 9	106
No Skin Sammy	107
The Feeding Frenzy	108
You Knew You Would Act This Way	110
XOXO	111
Circle Birds	112
Perfluster	114
Tasteful Nudes	116
Small Bones	117
No Good Mimi's	119
Bedside Manor	121
Tarantella	123
Fugazi	125
Long Straight Existentialist Hair	127
White Knuckle Weekends	129
Blue Eyes Are Cold	131
Punch and Judy	133
Coastal Evacuations	135
The Crowd Humbly Requests	137

Line Up The Animals

Somethings never change
A dusty throat, the theatre stage
Sits numb
In New York City
Looking glum
Sitting on the stoop you silly
Billy, open jackets are chilly
In New York City
Sit and stay man
A new command, the heads come in threes
Chewing gum
In New York City
What a pity
A helicopter light shines on the straw
Where a rolling castle falls
Washed away, turning gray
In New York City

You've been here once before
The pastry shop, the bloody floor
Sits cocky
In New Jersey
Looking tasty
Aren't you a little young?

It's a sad, silly Billy similar
In New Jersey
Blue in the face
Red hands every chance, occurring before noon
Feeling lazy
In New Jersey
Feeling worthy
I can die, I can die, I can die
But I'll never say I do
In New Jersey

Somehow this feels right
The open arms, the studded sides
Sits famous
In Las Vegas
Feeling aimless
Aren't you all washed up?
Even though it's dry
In Las Vegas
A black blotch
You got caught
You know very little of my life
Stories, painted in certain hues
It amuses you
You got the shock value
Feeling nameless
In Las Vegas

Have Nine Lives

A working waitress
When light's in total, manic depression
Hits the hair, it isn't fair
When it doesn't shine on yours
In Las Vegas

Tristan Buttigieg

Hero With A Thousand Faces

While the others were in trenches
And they ate the frozen meat
He ran out with his shotgun
Where he sure did pay the price
The Americans may have won the war
But the opposing has felt defeat
Burnt eyelids and shattered skulls
Stone bodies lay dead as ice

Jimmy's death was rough on him
He was the one who was any good
Understanding the true pain felt
That's how friendship is defined
Now serving tasks to the whorehouse queen
She feels he is inclined
Every-time he sees his son
He sees Jim where he once stood

Julia's life is a bitter drag
But don't leave a stone unturned
Father says he's a sideshow act
The best way to be unadorned

Have Nine Lives

Runaway and live with me
You won't have to live in fear
Fireplace crackles on the beach
Where they lay on the ocean's pier

The hero's mask is badly cracked
From the sights of a living war
The hero's mask is much too flimsy
For his friend is forever gone
The hero's mask is all too heavy
For the love that he feels for her

Nightmare Fuel

Sipping tea in the trash of a suite
Colored gloves on the roof where you lay
You sit still
What a thrill
A hard pill
To ponder every thought in your head

Circles grow in the case of a wire
The hot glow
Front row
Of the show attire
Smiles dread with cornered cheeks, the holy week
Do the deed, call it greed

Suckers salivate at the unknown chances
You play it cool
A living jewel
On the jumper chair
You sit hot, you big shot
Dreading every word with a sleek and muffled mutter

Have Nine Lives

The finite pieces in place, a dingy rat race
Fills up the hole
That every square will never fit in
Tough luck
You sitting duck
Up the ground with diamonds in full view

Send it off to the islands with surnames
Sitting still
One hundred hills
Of a face shaped out of burning
The sad truth
You set a booth
Full of dolls, hats, junk that says hug me

Bombay Sapphire

An open road I've traveled before
Fidget fighting through the halls
Scuffed enough to dance the mambo
Baked and flavored
All alone
With some old-world taboo of new waking spill bombs
A philosopher's song
Dreams, unholy
Groans, moans, in full throttle
The sound of a siren sitting loosely on land
With the canvas crying
Shrugging her shoulders
Swinging his head
Like sailors, straight in the air
Out in the open between you and the tracks
Don't mean a thing to me
Cold feet
The definition of culture
A main leading star throwing shadows on the floor
Captioned
Have you seen the accident outside?
No sir

Have Nine Lives

The clouds parting ways
Takes the world as a thief
In this Bombay Sapphire

Something in the air is off beat
You cover your blubber mask with sheets
What made us come to this mild city winter?
Blazed and stunning
In reverse
A whole ocean of oil under our feet
There will be blood at ten
Doves, tough
See you later alligator, the crippled stilts walk
Under poor lighting
Where it hurts the most
A tell-tale heart that was plucked by ravens
In this Bombay Sapphire

Tristan Buttigieg

All With Wildflowers

Soon
Tongues flicker lizard symbols
For esquires
The back light torch, a sudden sunrise
Army-sized
Not one saggy knee in the crowd
Whatever our souls are made of
All with Wildflowers

Tiny sticks swinging on the barrage of a drum
Plucked and pondered
An in-the-air-drab
With the residual sounds of children
Counting the hours
With frame-less glasses
All with Wildflowers

A bag of blowing
Make it royal
Throughout the city
Talking street
Beat, those green plastic figures

Have Nine Lives

Try not to laugh
Whistling in the graveyard for you
All with Wildflowers

Tristan Buttigieg

Haiku 1

Keeping the seat warm
Seeming right for each other
In their frozen graves

Low Hanging Fruit

Roadblocks scattered on the cutting edge of re-fine
Overall, bumper-cars
Do they have the same thing?
Coming to you live to this tailor-made present
Swaggered to the left
Making up the time by... (dot, dot, dot)
With old hungry ghost eyes
Can barely see outside, but the pain makes him jump
God forbid
With no snow in the trails
Shoulder to shoulder
Three peaches to the wind
Huddled for warmth
Do they see the same thing?
Sleeps standing up
Too cute to be restless?
A bleeding Susan on the last dog days
Table for two
From the wax to the wain
We will get no rain
Jumped like rabbits, stuffed in cabinets
Oh, the irony

Flowers blow in scorpion formations
You got something in your teeth
Learning how to walk straight
Blurry faces
Hello, hello
In the layered paint
Zapped by live wires
There's hope
There's light
But not looking for love
Do they move the same way?
Practiced faces in the mirror
He's lifeless
He's mindless
But looks peaceful to me
Whipping winds cold on a whipping skin kiss
It's dangerous
Contagious
And we're not worth the time
Do they do the same thing?
Spoon-fed the story
To your Low-Hanging Fruit

Seasons of Conejo

Recycled but screwed
Wearing red instead of green
Here come the butterflies
You can see this cloak of schemes
Oh doctor, oh doctor
Funny days
You can see his cougar skin
Money walks
Reaching up to the sky

Gingerbread collectors
A damsel in distress
Time after time
You look good without glasses
Hey mister, hey mister
With your hands on the side
Money talks
Very unstable for the first go around

Playing with balloons
Stepping on your shoes
No, you can't see how it goes

Tristan Buttigieg

Walking crocodile style
But every night...
Roses around the door
A sassy double take
He forgot to twirl
In a cameraman's scrapbook

Tears Don't Flow The Same In Space

Via Dolorosa
Five points to New York
Waiting for the colorless glass to bleed through nations
It's much too red
Too cold for a vest
Graves thrown at eagles in the entangled mesh
It's going to feel like Siberia
To be said, about the future's past

Sur la lune
They'll hang me at dawn
Stepping on groves, with the cement still wet
It's much too orange
A tinged, light strides
Just stand me up, and I'll do the rest
Reaching for the stars
To be carnage, on your bloody hands

Kings and queens
With broken scissor ends
Walk the blanket of cool frosted cat hairs

It's much too yellow
Bruised notes, with no crickets
Send me the leftovers
You blew it, you blew it
Technically she's mad
To be mellow, on the sunset strip

A babe in the woods
Busted petals made a crown
Billboard signs of amateur street crowds
It's much too green
Being buried in black
A dying winter flower shoves its head in the sand
Open wide, I can still drown
To be seen, by everyone

Je t'aime, Je t'aime
Hurricanes on the desk
A black moccasin slithers with stockings on her legs
It's much too blue
Baby faces made a tomb
Dodging the stairs under an open-necked version
Selling water in the winter
To be true, that you're always sad

Have Nine Lives

A la diaspora
An anchor drops deep
An oscillated sun shines bright but stays dull
It's much too purple
Chess pieces, stuck in circles
The traipse of hurdled names born yesterday
They can be like you and me
Eternal, on the ocean floor

The Humanoid Zoo

You know my heart is like glass
Blow me down, it's on the floor
You make it so obvious to me
Seasons change in the past of noon
A living snowflake
Prop
Drops on your shoes
Fists eclipsed
Drinking everything with those kissing blister lips
And watch that spider crawl
With a face, name, wink like chivalry

I take it in fully bloomed grains
A blurry-faced tragedy
Gliding lines will mark your demise
As a part of the plot, without blushing
Dumb in appearance, but wicked
Whoops
Spelled the front view of the pack going back

Taking bits and tips that you need
A jittery June, on the western front

Have Nine Lives

Causes a scene
Grey as seduction
Polly want a cracker?
No, but expected
You're feeding the birds trailing paint at their feet
Cold turkey
A look of the tin-man when she's still singing

Take it as a thing of the past
And how people would act
Very primitive
Spins and stops on this tornado
Go its life
It's green
Not sunburnt
Coming to you live with a head-lining no show
A fortune tellers dream
Stop
You only did it once, and you call yourself a king

Tinderbox

Knee-high and boneless
Made to fly
The notes of humility
Can't count
Can't shout
The cushion went down
And said tomorrow
The passage
The paths
With babies in your hands
Made to cry
The traipse of mixed bags
Don't care
Don't stare
The headlights turn black
Twisting through traffic
Sweating bullets in the womb
Willful
Wicked
A mess hall by night
Rock solid
Empty wallets
Drew a door to the board
Made to hide

And started knocking

HAIKU 2

Upper echelon
Ear-less collections of skin
A Hollywood script

The Geisha Parade

Opening the floodgates
Cross-fit
Counter-fit
The ID parade
Starts writing from scratch
Shows skin in the back
Haven't we met?
Turned red strolling pigeons
Gold mines
Flagellation
A mess hall by night
In the Geisha Parade

Blindfolded the cherries
Big heads
Pulling ears
The empire state
Turns a partial black
Jumps diving in ashes
Aren't you near?
Squeezed bricks to the light
Fine lines

Tristan Buttigieg

The sour grapes
A clean cut to the stem
In the Geisha Parade

A darling of technology
White caps
Saving face
Boiled in oil
Say it with a straight face
The wolves are at the door
Wouldn't you care?
Paper-trail of death certificates
Spellbound
The chimney sweep
Turned inside-out
In the Geisha Parade

BLUE RIBBON WINNER

Seven known destroyed
Too tough
Another ghost
What about all the clutter?
Stunned
Belly-up
Scattered coins in the river
Brought the city to laughter
Came to town
As a Blue-Ribbon Winner

The fog playing games
Too stiff
Wishing lists
Why do we flinch every-time?
Written
Just desserts
Kicking sticks to the flame
For white on rainy days
Cries alone
As a Blue-Ribbon Winner

Abandoned in the summer
Too fresh
Love like this
Scared to see your reflection?
Retreat
Rest easy
Your hands just skimmed the light
Writes frozen in the sand
Hello world
As a Blue-Ribbon Winner

Moonlighting @ Vogue

Double stacked at the time
Live wired from the start
Hatches
Madness
It shakes like disguise
Came back to the start of this dance
Falls smooth in its pursuit
Vendetta
To the notes
Starts poking at roses
Darting from tree to tree
Screams
Oh, French girls!
Oh, French girls!
Slicked to the cane
Blowing towards the bridges
Hall the tall one
Dipped in leather
Do you think this is funny?
Oh, Vassar!
Oh, Vassar!
Hands in your pockets
Smack dab in the middle
Shall we dance?

Tristan Buttigieg

Onto a fake, famous noon?
Runs a muck in Madison shoes
Throwing out some tea leaves

Haiku 3

The ping pong effect
A blasted iridescence
For pocket or purse

Gentleman Dreaming

A handful of ritzes
Locked stunted pockets
Cleansed
New life
Signed what a good star
Scream drinks, and they all come running

Business is booming
Friendly fire
Blissful peace
Shoving coats down our throats
Flies in the face
Favors, under the table

Dreams are born to the death of the past
Doesn't walk on tombs
And makes me impatient for the rest
Red mittens
The bucket jokes
A rushing hand that glides but doesn't touch
Declared to be the only way to heaven

SAME MOVES AS EVE

Sparks in the wind
What's next?
Swaying up and down the racks
And we laugh at the fact that your perfection is ruined
Button-down
Carved-out
I'm on your side of the room
Snowflakes
Fallen lighters
You crash-land through walls, and you swagger the ceiling
Leaving the home world intact
Dodging stones
Eskimo suits
Gliding roses from the heart
Squinting eyes see your ghost
Pokes
Spoke to you
Lady please don't stare
A new genetic pool
Tainted in the daytime
Like some new language, taught by animals
Up in the front-lines

Two steps out of civility
You cover my face to disclose your identity
And I knew you came because you smelled like roses
A checkered past
Falling under rainy weather
With its Mona Lisa smile
Where they turn sour in the end

BURIALS IN BULGARIA

All in, all that, but anything
Elephants sprawled across the back
Snake skins on the front
Rolling dice
Suzie fights
In sickness and in health
Cold
Golden
Collected in their palms
Gets gripped in the sand
What happened glowing eyes?
Nape stitched on the two o'clock hour
Peace to its ashes
Thirsty from the drowning
Black robes on the shore
Awkward smiles seen through the isles
And tight thighs in the angst of face-to-face
Pale
Criss-crossed
Your wet delirious wings
Her legs seeing stars
Quiet on the main boulevard

Stickfiguree

Wave it
Facing straight through the desert
Pledged death to the tear
Both faces
First capitol
Blue ocean drips down from his crown
Poignant the municipal
White tape
A heavy heart
Cemented in the street
Holding rubber necking counties
In a walking sign glow that comes off as green
Stellar
Inches away
Slideshows start when eyelids drop
Paused it on the perfect storm
In the shape of hitchhike
Ashes to ashes
A wild origami chase
Luck of the Irish engraved on his tomb
Where are all the artifacts?

Haiku 4

The high o'clock noon
So much for executions
Stretched atop the dead

Powdercake

In flocks of three
We would watch them collide
A weapon of fraction
Holding hands in the shape of their symbol
Rolling dice
Out of the box
A collection of swarms
Finger to the trigger
Cracks the haze
Singing hymns along the lake
On a violent Saturday night special
Loose scarves
Small rodents
Picking bones
Blasting rockets
They must think we're real heels
I'm done for
I'm poor
It's a destructive encore
Fingers smeared
Who knows too much?
Never lost
Never hidden

Porcelain Twins

Wilted like a lily
A forced color change
Sit straight
A bitter pill
On the wrong end of forty
Under what luck?
Eyes on the dart
Whistling notes in the dark
Two-faced
Infected
A slave to the sky
Does a leopard change his spots?
Under the heart of two Porcelain Twins

Out to have a taste
A big handful of stars
Boiled
Rogue
There's no thrusting room to spare
What's the possibility?
Another black eye
Making rude hand gestures
Trembling

Verified
The blind leading the blind
End of the morning
Blew a kiss when I'm sick
Onto the cheek of two Porcelain Twins

Metal Desk Furniture

A mime stood still
Turning sour for collection
Comes tramping
Cold shoulders
But was launched up too high
Clammed up
Slipping in
Under the role of a distraction
Make sure all her bones are broken
She's stunning
Why is some poured in unfamiliar places?
Hiding spots
Stenciled faces
Sticky glue the mountaintops
Breaking doors
Iron-clad alibi
Tied the clouds around with string
Swaying red every-time
Therefore, we are all dying here madam

Chalky Shale cats

Blue printed a smile
A passing landmark
Delicate notes play the keys of its waves
Gave the day
Performed the war
A requested encore broken in two
What's next?
And drained the ocean floor
Acting out a laugh
To those Chalky Shale Cats

Boys go at it
Her head laying low
A definitive host
Just a glitch among the millions
Thereafter
Three times
A candid attempt
Threaded with teases
On the night of the fire
With those Chalky Shale Cats

Have Nine Lives

Tries to apologize
Why we?
Before they traveled
With time touching tender spots to quicken the process
Never on board
Never be wholly
Dragged away in their white satin sheets
Adored
Up roared
Gliding to the streets when we needed them the most
Always taking turns
Those Chalky Shale Cats

Foam Hole Rooms

Walking through their eyes
Now what of your face?
Starts to melt
Motions the shattered
A violent fit of rage
Whimpering worries
Got caught turning heads
Bestowed the crown by accident
Raised from denial
A twirling hypnosis
Gathered in tangled nets

Clear nebulous tint of the blackest ink
Has your light burned up in smoke?
Jumpers
Tiptoeing
Pointing to the wrong end of forty
Conformist confusion
With the sign reading ellipses
Tapping thimbles
Raising silhouettes
Absent people who are in distress

Haiku 5

Moons follow the dark
An alley not discovered
The Broadway stage set

Lacuna Fortuna

You do the best in crisis situations
A joke heard in Manhattan
Dresses and changes to a unique point of view
Intimately kept
When you sleep, does it matter?
The slow-cooked features make a headway for the lights
Running out of time
Too hot to settle
Too cold for me to stay
While banned
Holds his own paradise
Venoms the stop of every single block
An expected hurt when I try
From channel to chalk, we're considered filthy
Am I naturally supposed to love you?
Doubly so
How fast it goes by
How can anybody ask?
Mere trepidation of the earth

Rainy Season in The Andes

Piece the frames one by one
The sounds of blood sailing over
Lays her eggs
Postpones the struggle
Told that you're bold
That you're displaying through the windows

Show me what a dollar looks like
An expected hurt when I try
Shakes to the rhythm
A rushing intensity
Plush and full
The cracked folds of envelopes

Overflowed with gasping clasps
Sweaty hands address hieroglyphics
Eye to eye
A look alike fashion
Giving off heat
The one cause of assistance

Tristan Buttigieg

Cardinal badges on familiar walls
Signatures roar in a class of their own
The start of this dance
With cemented features
To a third world war
Where it takes the face of a human
And now we've mixed real cotton candy

COLOR IT WITH FIRE

Mumbles on the railway
Turning space lesion pale
Honey dipping low in the sky
Blushes feeling obliged
Ran off to the ships
Leaving burnt tire tracks
Colored in with fire

Banded lambs in phony shams
Acting out the werewolf
Primary thunder
Secondary frost
No blondes allowed for feasting
Colors shifting
Wrote down the reactions
Bright glowing faces
In the softened ground
Colored in with fire

More and more
I give you go-go eyes
Smeared a kiss

Icy, spicy tears
Hiding temptation
And showing his fear
Collapses on the highway
The bleeding reflection
The arrow heads fall flat
In honor of the lights
Colored in with fire

Kamikaze file lines
The sideways serenity
Turning knobs
Renaissance lambs
Stamped onto their vulnerable crowns
Sickled souls
They lower the coffin
Criss-crossed at the drop of a hat
Playing dead in the winter
Colored in with fire

Mirrors the nameplate
Emotions on the mending
The human roars
Where the one rose has thorns
Cream colored

Have Nine Lives

Teeth chipping
Where we pick at their brains
Due to the snowstorm
Where we left before nightfall
Colored in with fire

In His Sunday Best

Fictional, biblical characters other than virgins pull all the stops
Flames assert brunet barleys under total control in cursing gestures
To that malicious monarch, the watchmen stare from a distance
Named Cesar Ludd, because of his brilliance gone ballistic

Metal tentacles other than ocean snuffed lumber hammers
The middle-class version motions his men to raise anarchy
A shadow of rebellion, stamped on their private, vulnerable skull caps
The old-fashioned version, gathering his amplified cavalries
Oh, what a comforting presence, when laboring men start to snap

It's Only Good For Business

Close and clouded
A dying swindle farce
Center-stage begins
With the exchange of breaking continents
Show me a smile
The same salt on your tongue
Big evening stars
A candy moon to the head

Daydreams on the stage
A muzzle to the mouth
Existing in the hall
The sanity of home-grown soul
Split with screams
Snaps a sneer with his strings
Flipping ocean tides
Singing with compassion

Blue whistles sail across
Constructed to be cuddled
A watered-down puppet
With a crinkled conflict forced out of snooze

Among the swarming
On a rare, bright occasion
Messages of a profile
Commercialized from the start

Consolation twin reunion
A canopy of numbers
Molded to be chosen
Starts playing the crocodile
Standing still
Freezes around the bend
One-armed navigators
In the antique picture screen

Haiku 6

Haunting bare tones stand
His free ghost flutters with him
The woods with no hum

Polishing The Marble

Another sun rises
You're better off than me
All in hiding
Always so trusting
Windows your feelings
Returning as far as the sins of home

Laughing in the corner
Forced you off for the remaining time
Cold-winter blows
Passing notes
Only if you're willing
Won't you now share your body?

A speaking revolver
Insects without a stinger
Thought of as a lie
Continues to cry
Voices changing color
And why do you cry attack!

SUGAR RAW

Holds out his hands
Dread overflowed the scenarios
Dropped enough to know
And flows powder to the wind
Hot-blooded
Red desert
The real prisoners have escaped
Leaning heads
Calling cards
What button should I press?

Sunshine's raining
Where we laugh and we shiver
Cozied up to the sky
And settled infinite scores
But dress me up before I do it
Colorful canyons
Black letter badges
Hungry rumors spread around in their boots
Street shows
Quivering smoke
You can almost cut it with a knife
Childish at heart

And watches him die

Red letter warnings
Skipping sectors in the metro
The sign reading ellipses
Highlighted in postures across steep rolling hills
Bitter seeds
Bended knees
Random constellations shine bright but stay dull
Occupants in ashes
Melted makeup frowns
Used by shutting off the sanity
Knowing nobody has to get hurt

WE FEAST @ 3:08

Views the surfaces as it becomes our everything
Arriving at the agitated hands
Between the lines
By the numbers
Felt a fire across your lips
Spraying hearts on your legs

Splattered on the nape of your neck
Turns the innocent into sand
Settling scores
Seven downstairs steps
With their ship boats that sink
Ruling on an iron beach chair

Surgical kisses through the poplin flesh
Overwhelmed with planets in the sky
Mixed in
Their own stunts
Long awaiting for you to speak
The skeleton will do just fine

Kilroy Was Here

Blue wetland slit
An anxious wave of sirens
The misty ocean commotion
The first chuckle to your lips
Seven standing without collapse
Breaking knees
Angry faced
Peaceful clouds wrapped in his lightning
The dream in front of you

A one-time touch
Kissed the next life goodbye
Making the blood disappear
Says a trauma has been smeared
Cold treks
Ugly faces
A growing respect for an unknown last name
The dream in front of you

Lighting his bombs
The fatal glass frame
The least suspecting element

Shifting eyes in the buried kingdom
Flickered fish
A societal ghost
Missiles tied to the noises of heartache
The dream in front of you

Tristan Buttigieg

It's Almost Funny

There's this whole debacle
An upper cosmic shade
Bad apples
Most-wanted
A childlike wonder
Seeing the physical street
Falling weak to your presence up close
Tight knit
Stands locked
A newborn obsession
Sealing trillions of daunting sequences
The premature night
Learning the language of distant cousins
Sprawled like a bird
Her manikin like hands
Translating a long, spreading resolve
The emotional ends standing tall
For the meek
So deep it seems to turn
The appetizing stains
Resting my eyes when you're still speaking
Barring any unforeseen blinking
Unfortunately fighting when she's still golden
Never wanted glory

Have Nine Lives

Or any purple hearts
Held a white flag up in the casket
Wrapped in their chains
Isolated in the quarry
Imagining how we carried each other
Light as a zeppelin
Antics planting words
Stripping the tease
Collapsing colorless in one piece
With no protection from the ground

Tristan Buttigieg

The Commodore's Shack

Glass tears packing on a pale spring morning
Tights turns avoided the land from screaming
Broke his fall
An ashen-faced mirage
Pounded out an intense smile
Arms crying through the windows
Damp and ditzy
Inside voices
Gardening any false pretenses
The obvious things in life
At the Commodore's shack

Pale bunk twines wake from watercolor dreams
Shot down a bleak purpose, to the next extreme
Born with a future guide
Giving it out like candy
Five different specimens
Housed in
A muzzled reaction
Positioned beacons split across their face
Jarring sunlight
Shrieking blue ruin
The obvious things in life

At the Commodore's shack

Jumping doors lazy on account of their smirks
Conveyed enough time to fight for your heart
Comedic faces
An up-and-coming coat
Secured the growing fights
Shut the lipstick for the night
Simple calls
Walks away with half the blue doubt
Was only valid because of the lost hope
The obvious things in life
At the Commodore's shack

Tristan Buttigieg

SAVING FACE

Glides down headfirst
Lights a presence made of marble
Blew their spirits to the ground
And named you the announcer
Old news
Backstabbing
Knocked the tchotchkes to the ground
Colored dreams
A played past
The coldness of one's shadow

All clear turn-downs
The sideways skid marks
Spreading contacts through the wind
And said nothing but rebellion
Hugging heads
Fallen cans
The moon charting the sky
Cross-eyed
Pulling teeth
And sounding the alarms

Haiku 7

Saturday's invoice
The repetitive motions
A unique cadence

Little White Shoes

Broke down the doors
The rank and file
Making a fish scream for water
Spraying exes
Conned a cunning surprise
But prefers it cool to keep him awake
A comforting curse
The pressing ultimatum
Slowly deprived of heat on her face
Punctured holes
A take-it-or-leave-it
Weighing out the odds
As a weird romance
Events unfold in the wake of an accident
Tapping to ask if it can come in
Old roses
Baby-faced
The afternoon identity
A long, crashing sting
Dreaming they could sing
Shot down
Hung up in the hills
And performed for the evening
As a key to the city

Have Nine Lives

If only they could talk
With anything but heavenly trailing off
Seeking out the fortunate things

Tristan Buttigieg

Wind Chimes On The Far North Side

No photos show her face
Small-minded tears fall flat with features
Wounded plumes
Seagulls in the night
Sends a dove dodo in my direction
One scrounging in the puddle
One flash in the pan
A running man with his pants on the floor

Nuance to nuance
Blue noons ascending throughout the city
Banking a cause
And signing his rhymes
Cracked sexual stone being pressed to death
Two mural the postures
Two screaming for air
Of a light nightmare moving swiftly in the reigns

Swallowing the lines
Scrambling through the revolving doors
String in a box
Nobody felt the threat

Have Nine Lives

Of crystal gifts circling the sunrise
Three Hollywood scripts
Three shaking when you sit
Countless whispers heard in the crowds

Our Usual Song

Won through this world themselves
A penny a year to a prompted paranoia
His is the dark knight
Yours is the white knight
Scrolled the mess
And beat with his yarn
Come get me
Come get me
You look like a bucket of uncooked meat
Shy sun
Dead wringers
The scented lighted guise
In the odd wad of castrated structures
And thought that they could fly
Comes playing
Comes pointing
Death inclines where life kept us in stitches
Bowed heads
Kicking mountains
The bullet hole leaves
Playing the part of a fish out of water
Half decent for the pickings
Come crying
Come crying

Have Nine Lives

The straight jokes turned to dust
Washed enough of those trickled muses
Come dirty
Come clean
There must have been some suspicion?
One size later
The usual display
Kept cold
Kept comical
Found the gold of the prairie
You might as well take a hammer to the face
Who dreamed that they could smile
On his routine flight
Dragging on the floor
Cross-eyed to the wind
And to think it was made for a silly like me

Tristan Buttigieg

CHOKING NICKIE'S AND DEEP EDDIE'S

Sitting on the doorstep, drinking down the medicine
Boot prints been bought for the rats
Kicking out the cobblestones, sailing through bourbon seas
Pull, swing, and hit with your ax

Sending out the firearms, making up the storybooks
The chair's been thrown across the room
Yelling at the deputy, wave around his Tommy piece
His two fingers sideways with his thumb

Cautious black hands, flatfoots, and heads drenched with dew
Have all come knocking at your door
Hang the rocks around his hands, and kick his legs in between
Show this fool what you got

Climbing up the purple ranks, and rusty diamonds in the rough
We'll talk about it when he leaves
The Brooklyn brawls are here to stay, and Manhattan's mitts are coming off

Have Nine Lives

Lucky Charlie's turning in his grave

Gaunt faces in the park, souls you left a head start
To be holding hands with the devil
The talking drinks starts to ding, and rushing highways to your ring
You're doing what you do from the start

The triangle has broken apart, and now becomes a hundred dots
Right from the two equal signs
You're hit, you clench, and then you scream, and then you crawl because you think
This is going to be headline news
Rusty bullets hit the side, and painted hands will recline
Right on the side of your chair
A jack of trades, and girls will play, your ticket biscuit's been erased
I'll have a table just for one

Tristan Buttigieg

Fast responder

Teary-eyed
Too royal
Checked off all the boxes
It's tough
A range of colors
Waited for an introduction
Shocked night
Second-hand
Gave way to his passing
In blanch
Switched the riffs
When waves were once used
Noisy tombs
Held up their umbrellas
Flashed with gold, and pressed lightly in return
A character in itself
Different measures for her cursing
Shot the sky for silence
With no crosses buried

Don't Cry Over Spilled Juice

Finger ringlets stocked of spacious holes and volcano spews, dark crimson red, to purple tints, to bright cherry blossoms, permanently looking back at you, the skin won't grow back, more open sores for more open cries

The stomach has been punctured, and the bubble wrap has been popped, I know the feelings of inanimate objects, dead and waking in and out of consciousness, crying over spilled juice

Sugar slinks in the form of snakes, including vital intentions through endocrine's troy horse, and breaks the layer of brink and stone with your legs, one by one, the toes get cold, walking over spilled juice

Manic circles within the results of bombastic cages jumping up and down, fist in hand, for the next battle. Tenement buildings packed and shipped according to the time of day, the blue overcrowd, the green compete, but the red is shyly standing in the rails, crying over spilled juice

Tristan Buttigieg

Stick With Me Lazarow

You're a man with a dream in your childhood years
Scissored out
Throwing pennies
All that glitters isn't gold
Blasting badges on familiar walls
With no part in the plot
The start of this dance creates a river of tears

Expired like a flower
Failed health takes the maker
And we weep
Taking the shine off of yourself
A monster of the night
With shards in your dreams
Must the child be arrested?
Praying to the azure chrome skies of the one true savior

Throwing newspaper prints at the graveyard bones
Scrambled
En route

Have Nine Lives

Separate piles of ashes
Shining light through the sky
Through the popcorn raindrops
Keeps the kids
Borrowed them only for the night

Moved to the east coast to marry my true bride
A haunting ghost
To their plastic displays
Spinning wheels
Missing pages
Walking through each other's eyes
Paint brushed lust between the lines
Little did we know that we were blood on the run

Heaves a loss
A dedicated depression
Shows death doesn't wait
Wearing thorns
Steals the form
Of a three-dimensional scheme
The ravine breaks for parents of two

The injections of nighttime slashings
Struggled
Bludgeoned
Looking ancient as usual
Comforting an old-fashioned flame
Time chips at the saw, and the sand timers sand starts to drain
Daughter's husband dies, and Gracie's gone insane
Whatever happens to me kid
I'll always be with you

Haiku 8

Solo survivor
Weighed the same after bloodshed
The violent lakes

Tristan Buttigieg

Portuguese Man O'War

Swoon says the sun
Vigil dripping between the lines
Give us a kiss
Bouldered and blocked
Faintly stepping onto the heart that spells choose
Gouged the bust
And made the first move
Skirting around
And found the weakest spot
The black backdrop peering on its sides
Double tides
The doe-eyed soul
Removed its shoes
Clinging onto the champions of destructive shadows
Blue globule double
The fumbling of the fire
Made the first move
A beautiful woman sitting idly on the docks
Keeping the matches dry

The Great Circus Fire

Boy
Come forced says the light
Merry
Merry
The pines slither slow
Shuffling through the richest skin
Sinner
Sinner
White recedes the rain
The bird hasn't crowed yet
Launched a dominant fire
Platoons
Platoons
A sunset gap in the road
Caution to the time
Corrupted by color
Sold
Told the cheeks say hello
Placed the tongues on the steps
Jumped from zero to five
Girl
Black botches the wind
Drifting with the current

Tristan Buttigieg

Where the old whistles go
Fine fitted
Fine fitted
Her majesty waved a frown
One-night star
A dominant vein
Digestive minds
An untrained ear
Do you see the moon over Soho?

Round-Topped Stela

Thought of as another
Lucky
Destructive
Killed the tutor of the man
Stopped and stuttered
There's anguish in this light
Fought
Frolicked
This is what angels looks like

She doesn't come changed
The brightest travel
The darkest search
This hand is pure
With a funny line in the play
Haste to vacate
There's anguish in this light
Strait-laced
Bitter taste
This is what angels look like

They're not going to need it now

Tristan Buttigieg

Changed his lines
They had nine lives
He'd look funny on my table
And quit doing the majestic
The boy is a kill joy
There's anguish in this light
A new rule
In five swift moves
This is what angels look like

The intense moment of connection
Two dogs on his shoulders
Twenty days out at sea
They got a lot of chutzpah
Distributed in equal rations
There's anguish in this light
This one walks
And beseeched to the fall
This is what angels look like

MALADY MELADY

All the colors in his face
A golden survival
Plays a note as his last
A little rain must fall
Pioneering every ground
Make me pretty
A pity invite
Shaped out is a soul of common speech
Slow sleep
A fox trot
Get to work you jerk
Show me the death mask
I wouldn't call it flawless
Hum what I heard
Made the candles dance
Crippled promise
No nonsense
Trails a colored coated sheen
Your money's no good here
With their head in the clouds
Labored breathing
Jutted grease
Working hard or hardly working?
Sunk the silhouette

Tristan Buttigieg

Retreating in their newspapers

Mason's Ashtray

A catacomb of synonyms
Handsome
Verbose
Being played like matches
An old New York school blue on the corner
Cleared the cobwebs
The first caiman
Did you trickle down a cornered street?
Taxed the road-map
Stitched a trip made of gold
Blood lust
Filled the cups
Along rows of identical gravestones
Waiting to take flight
It's a working man's game, belonging to children
A sunset gap in the road
Dusted
Screeching
Lightning's backwater rising
False advertising
You may spill on the floor of her stomach
Persona Non Grata
A vulture's mold

Souls jumped from something fierce
Weathered and orange busting through the shades
How long would it take?
Adding insult to injury
The widows walk
Black umbrellas
A virtual line
Running like they had a purpose
In the morning

HOUSE AT HAST

Stick with clicks
A joke to cope
Bravado
Barricado
Won done by whim
How's the weather up there?
Shrunk like a tortoise
A ticket of leave
Spread his legs, and said so-so to the sea
If need be
A film fantastic enough for a glowing masked parade
How could you cry for a normal person?
Smoke me a note
A go-getter
Distinctive hats when you've done something bad
And the murder that you planned
White gauges
The willows
A twinkle in the mountains
Forests of insults
The walk home
Prepare to wear the darkness that we once defended
How could you cry for the individual?

Extra Sevilla

The first circuit
Made a modest house
The furthest fringe
A pocket full of traits
Right as rain
A ring of kids
Soap in the blood
Slept in the same bed
Blue and pompous
A surge of castles
Hysterics on the stairs
The one-hundred-year storm
Go figure
A winner
Blowing flowers red and raw
Namby-Pamby
Gun shy
A soft-spoken tongue
The knife wish
Zippered lisps
Have you seen the latest roast?
A leading lady
A madman parading
Caution to the children playing

Have Nine Lives

Guess who's walking home

Tristan Buttigieg

Haiku 9

Glass hands backing off
Shoulder to shoulder
On looking closer

No Skin Sammy

Black and decker
Soiled doves
Went away with the nerves
Came to me with spots stuck to his neck
Let the lilies out
There are ladies present
Waved out by the cast
And brought on by static
Whisky tears
A peep show
Wallows in his stable calamities
Busted tattles
Beguiled lines
Carried their weapons into town
A pioneered grimace
Intuitions of the dead
A maiden's sultry voyage
Didn't know how to support his tuft
The only ones to declare them saints

The Feeding Frenzy

Haunted the bare tone standing
The independent floats
Aligned all the stars with no words
In the Feeding Frenzy

Short water rests
The woods with no hum
His free ghost flutters with him
Breathing heavily on their backs
In the Feeding Frenzy

How could you ask then?
A distracted middle name
Daggers spoke in the evening of the coops
Looking for a back-scene
In the Feeding Frenzy

The gift of wires
A ring-around survival of the folded couples
Fell back on the coast
False hope

With a sheltered clamor to a matador's speech
In the Feeding Frenzy

Slamming doors smoked as he provoked
A delight in someone's downfall
The distinctive sounds of bowling balls
With wondrous tears to the moon
In the Feeding Frenzy

What goes around comes around
Fidelity across the stream
Stiff and sure as the hush of cadavers
Think about all the mean things
In the Feeding Frenzy

You Knew You Would Act This Way

Shadows in chateaus
Called the red-hot community
Four-corners
Salted daddies
A strange thunder in the world
Sweet-lady underscore
Called out the vaporous sway
A severe wish
Limited lips
The dust of a non-believer
An animal in its prime
The broadened physical foibles
Glass animators concur the mountains
Calling them diluted nobles
A bolt of water, beautiful but deep
The primitive outweighing the present
Etched a glance
The second in command
An unconscious clutch to the face
Filtered with nostalgia
Termed the petrified street
The mortal soil
The black natural margins
Making the main picture your rainbow

XOXO

Small items in the news
A living testament to the sick
Last chapters
Bad actors
Similar children trace on the windows
XOXO
Famous last words
Broken dust on the cusps
Organic hacks in the fashion of actions
Swimming in the same awkward position
You know, XOXO
A legendary evil
The grapes grounded with blood
The color of love
Propose that it does rain
A king and his peeling paint
Unsavory
The winds of a disinterest
Why don't you just go die already?
With the intention of its mystery
XOXO

Circle Birds

Suitable performances beam in the warranties
Strong desires
Rubbing knees
Enhanced phantoms in the muddled methods
Take it as gospel
The motel matches
Rushed to its most relevant test
The decapitated run
Cut of the clouds
For authority and for fun
Give her all the bolts you got
Running on rooftops
The collective cards
A change within the picture
A change within the song
Forlorn
The perpetual glance
Dirty liaison
The cryptic son
Pronged a heart in the limit of some faith
Dead on arrival
The monarch's daughter
Fighting sideways
While he runs with his gun

Have Nine Lives

Attack its stand
Performed the tender venues until the end

Tristan Buttigieg

Perfluster

Gained less of the lust
A bruised null in his yarn
Look it up punk
The rave reviews
Over poured in the heat
Tickled you pink
The foreign affairs
Fell like a straight suit
The one-thousand-yard stare
Same goes to Perfluster
Too late for the news-stand
A dusty cosmetic
The humorous distance
Look at them run
Crushed candy underfoot
Stacked high
Stood naked
The bare-bones privilege
The immovable string
Same goes to Perfluster
The nominated cause
Balanced like a seesaw
The forefront of six dates
A tired sky

Direct estimates
Why is everything so trivial?
The same goes to Perfluster
How slow is the end?

Tasteful Nudes

A flash interest
Losing their innocence
Socially amazing
A messy, muddy feeling of thanks
A lost care
Cull
Called the calculated cult
There's no one there, but all the applause
White roses
Red angels
The palpitating stars
Breezy
Taboo
Beauties in the same clothes
Veritable feasts
Their gills glowing bright
Say grace
Over-casted
A bad photogenic
The sheep with no skin
Silent surfs in the night
A bandit in the sun
Chased like a wet rat

Small Bones

The indisputable truth
Same day came the swine
Dissolved
Came the brawl
Two ships made of steel
Same night at the races
The panicked separation
While conquering their fears
The bitter blood surrounded by spoons
What a loon
Either lucky or lightheaded
The half-broken vines
Mandated
Half-full
The rosy champagne turfs
What's a jerk without benefits?
Their smiles growing old
All caught up
A coat of different feathers
Knowing they could sit there and laugh
With small bones
Caved-in
The corner stone
Laying softly on his belly

Tristan Buttigieg

Tilted head on the stick
The same afternoon party
Held high
The strained lights
The same corroded jewel
Same hour came the anchor
Looking human as usual
With small bones

No Good Mimi's

Picnic by the highway
The infernos that follow
Withered moons
The slow moves
The very same cemetery
Long squawk of the flute
Fast times
Shining eyes
The swindle of swank redemption
Same commander sang the blues
Little baby fortnight
The same morose repair
Receded
Frustrated
An often paralyzing white
Sucking honey from their veins
Overflowed by the four points
Witchcraft
Counteract
Flying blindly in the shows
Noted only in soft sedation
Animosity in the background
A total damnation
The survivor's croon

Tristan Buttigieg

Catching something that's not even there

Bedside Manor

Double-parked
The sweet source
Compare me to the cult
The unchecked paths
A crooked swan dance
Her bedside manor
Obtuse
Untouched
A silent sky at its best

Seaside comforts
The oracle of the bend
Some that don't go to heaven
Did she ever make a sound?
The faded glass frames
Lazy loathes in the trees
His bedside manor
Silted
Flamboyant
Dusted lashes in the heat

The disappearing act
Mashed

Coming quietly for a kiss
Witnessed
Assumed
The height of the false boom
Her bedside manor
Pretend
Assumed
The flowers that came apart

The accurate portraits
All the low-needy years
Sprawled singing a show
Bristled woes in the thorns
The promised miracle growth
Their bedside manor
It's not that great
You fill in the rest

TARANTELLA

The prominence of the day
You can't afford to dream
Came clean
Came hungry
Light orders of the warmth
Normally here
They're bowling up there
Ruined heirs
The assassin's occupado
The expired wounds of the hour
Poor
Deformed
The outdoor torpedo
Slept the night
The pretty papers
Could tell time by reading the scars on her arms
Danced the ornate pave
Repetitive
Pretend
The fatal distribution
Executive protection
It took one person with a mission
Natural beauty
The fire in the flowers

Tristan Buttigieg

The rhythms
Art of violet
Stranded in the kitchen sink
Desert wisps
The rusted buddy circle
The bridge between two worlds
Just for the sake of debate

FUGAZI

Came down the dismount
The framed bedside retreat
Night bombs
Dried fruit
The small bands of rain
Thirsty trash
The wide birth
Spilled the muddle of his speech
Twisted arms
Blooms in the park
The first battle of the buy
No signals
What humor
After-cry
The survivors
All the cold things first
The silent sounds of the house
While she fell like a dancer
Comatose
Came running
The secondhand swim
A sheltered reminder of a whistle in the wind
Hey baby in blue, how are you?
The solitary planes

Tristan Buttigieg

That's where all the strangers go

Long Straight existentalist hair

One-punched pilot
The hands of well wishes
Shook up
Shortsighted
The tragedy of the commons
Bellwether
Bar banter
The triple worldwide boost
Old lights
The dark horse
The rolled-up paper planes
Stiff upper lip
The details that don't exist
Jerk with the nose
The motor-run speed-bump
The split-ended heels
Heavy heads
The bloody rings
Their names became the byword
Cast ashore
The divided shadows
Deemed too hard for the chase
Came way to the grandstand
Red shimmer

Bad tidings
A greedy tyrant with the eyes
Queen of spire
A molten deluxe
The diluted gain of an honor
Busted tracks
The abandoned shop
The heat of the noon
Beyond the pale
A day-time screening
Running silly in their boots

WHITE KNUCKLE WEEKENDS

Tour de force
The bread and the circus
High tide
Home theatrics
The discrete modes of depression
Lumbago
No takers
The walking wounded
The predominant race
Cake face
Chopping blocks
The mirrored rocking horse
Teeth in the paint
The skeleton staff
The necessary evils
A creature of habit
Hop along
Put up your dukes
And walked away like the gangsters do
The stand-alone cloud
Dragged through the roses
Beautiful
Delusional
I can't read your mind

Tristan Buttigieg

Because I'm legally blind
An honorable mention
The final killing blows

BLUE EYES ARE COLD

Slugged sands in ten bars
Battle royale
The order of the express
Freed the beast
The child was once sweet
How far up in the air?
She came back for a kiss
Sixth show level of man
Spilled the wine
The motherhood of false standings
A crack in its trap
Transitioned like a monk
The champion in the dark
Rummaged in the sun
The last play-back curse
Shmey drey
The bloody feet of the trade
Split down
The souvenirs
Shredded curbsides
The main branches of a tree
Thieving iron lines
Inventions of the woven
The immovable forces

Regular skeletons
Familiar territories
The cool breath of the outsider
Planned liar
The new-day essence of another child
Soldiered-on
The cultural danger
Chased the faces into the unknown hours
Hands in patterns
The animate sources
Collided
Collected
Dreamed of maneuvers
Loosing when it matters
The sliced attack stands still in the heat
Feeble loins
The fishes in the fan
The wheelhouse of ten choices
Punched a heart through the ocean
Considered a lightweight
Mistaken by all the beautiful sounds

Punch and Judy

Ripping tides
Rushing into silence
The highlight of first mornings
Smooth asylum
Happy exile
All the main voyages
The tundra in their eyes
A quicker draw
The vandalized stars
Look at them laying
Dropped the third midnight stay
Wobbled
Cakewalks
The chocolate box ensembles
The howling croons of the young
Tired tracks
The violent lakes
Do you want me to cry for you?
The silent machines
Heavy hands
The mechanical laughs
No scam ma'am
What luck that we have
The superhuman act

Tristan Buttigieg

Of retrieving the dead

Coastal Evacuations

Released as a virgin
The home-front corrosion
Lone echo
Flat-footed
The pulse of old things
Cute cut
The first blush
A hanging rose on the door
An unparalleled hell
Sleepwalker
Fast talker
The monastery of the mind
Propped knight
The after-fight
Naming an attraction
The last standing ovation
Punch-drunk
You whipping posts
All the motions in a picture
Sketch to sketch
A lonely post
A cloud with the down arrow
An orchestral crescent
Thick as thieves

Tristan Buttigieg

The calm of summer
Cotton mouth
The baby-switch
The showcased color
A strategic case

The Crowd Humbly Requests

De la force a la force
The flawed shapes of death
One drum
Second verse
The seventh nightly shroud
Upper crust
Cold shavings
The accurate portraits
The dominating card
Blood suckers
Strange beauty
The demonstrative suit
Forced grins
Damaged goods
The walk-through hit
The enormous sway
Lost loves
En plein air
All the last resting places
Suiting smells
Quiet scenes
The handicapped spot
All the cosmetic mistakes
No hesitation

Knowing that they'll get attacked
Circle bound
Background
The neutral heat of the noon
The background violin
Too tired to be inspired

ABOUT THE AUTHOR

Tristan Buttigieg is a singer-songwriter, musician & poet. Just as he felt his predecessors of the poetic and musical revolutions of the early to mid-20th century accurately portrayed, he's someone who firmly believes that the objective of art should be equivocal and unrestrained, while always capturing inspiration from the genuine day-to-day occurrences of human life, blended in with the hidden depths of the subconscious mind. Along with engaging in his writing, Tristan has additionally released seven brand new collaboration albums titled "Bubbles On The Ceiling"[2018], "Einstein's Garage" [2018], "Parallel 33" [2018], "Roar of Time" [2019], "Cosmos Colossus" [2020], "House of Hast" [2021], & "Jack of Habits" [2021]. He currently resides in Bucks County, Pennsylvania.

www.ingramcontent.com/pod-product-compliance
Lightning Source LLC
Chambersburg PA
CBHW062110290426
44110CB00023B/2774